Gospels of Mercy

12 Steps to the Love of God

by
Fr Adrian Graffy

All booklets are published thanks to the generous support of the members of the Catholic Truth Society

CATHOLIC TRUTH SOCIETY
PUBLISHERS TO THE HOLY SEE

Contents

All rights reserved. First published 2015 by The Incorporated Catholic Truth Society, 40-46 Harleyford Road London SE11 5AY Tel: 020 7640 0042 Fax: 020 7640 0046. This edition © 2015 The Incorporated Catholic Truth Society.

ISBN 978 1 78469 095 3

Introduction

Christians treasure four different accounts of the life of Jesus, which are called gospels. The Gospel of Luke gives a rich portrait of Jesus, which highlights above all his meetings with ordinary people and his teaching. The twelve passages in this booklet, which we are calling 'gospels of mercy', are taken from Luke's work, and give a flavour of the whole gospel. They are chosen to help you get to know something about Jesus as he really was, what he taught and what he did. Jesus came not to condemn, but to forgive. He came to call not the just but sinners. He is a witness to the reality of God and of the mercy of God.

The gospel texts are quoted from the Jerusalem Bible, with small adjustments in line with the original Greek.

1

Good News to the Poor

LUKE 4: 16-22

Jesus came to Nazareth, where he had been brought up, and went into the synagogue on the sabbath day, as was his custom. He stood up to read, and they handed him the scroll of the prophet Isaiah. Unrolling the scroll he found the place where it is written: 'The spirit of the Lord has been given to me, for he has anointed me. He has sent me to bring the good news to the poor, to proclaim liberty to captives and to the blind new sight, to set the downtrodden free, to proclaim the Lord's year of favour.' He then rolled up the scroll, gave it back to the assistant and sat down. And all eyes in the synagogue were fixed on him. Then he began to speak to them, 'This text is being fulfilled today even as you listen.' And he won the approval of all, and they were astonished by the words of grace that came from his lips.

Good News to the Poor

This gospel of mercy tells us so much about Jesus and his purpose. Luke reports that Jesus, after preaching in various other places in the region of Galilee, returns to the town of Nazareth, where he was brought up. He visits the synagogue on the Sabbath day according to Jewish custom, and he reads from the Bible. These are the first words of the adult Jesus which Luke records. They have great importance. They are taken from the Old Testament book of the prophet Isaiah.

Jesus is in fact applying these words to himself. He is claiming that the Spirit of God is with him, and with him for a purpose. The people whom he wishes to reach are first of all the poor. 'Good news to the poor' is the slogan of Christianity. It really is good news that God exists and that God's fundamental attitude to us is understanding love, mercy and compassion. Jesus proclaims liberty to captives, new sight to the blind, freedom for the downtrodden, and the favour of God. All the gifts of God are positive and they are designed to assist those in the greatest need. They are designed for us in our need. The message of the good news proclaimed by Jesus is for all of us today, and particularly for those feeling alienated and lost, those who see life as a bad joke, a time of pain and suffering ending in death, and that's it.

• Does this message of good news seem incredible to you, or might it just be true?

• What difference would it make in your life if you welcomed the gospel with an open mind and heart?

2

Jesus calls Peter

Jesus said to Simon Peter, who was a fisherman, 'Put out into deep water and pay out your nets for a catch.' Simon replied, 'Master, we worked hard all night long and caught nothing, but if you say so, I will pay out the nets.' And when they had done this they netted such a huge number of fish that their nets began to tear, so they signalled to their companions in the other boat to come and help them; when these came, they filled the two boats to sinking point.

When Simon Peter saw this he fell at the knees of Jesus, saying, 'Leave me, Lord; I am a sinful man.' For he and his companions were completely overcome by the catch they had made; so also were James and John, sons of Zebedee, who were Simon's partners. But Jesus said to Simon, 'Do not be afraid; from now on it is people you will catch.' Then, bringing their boats back to land, they left everything and followed him.

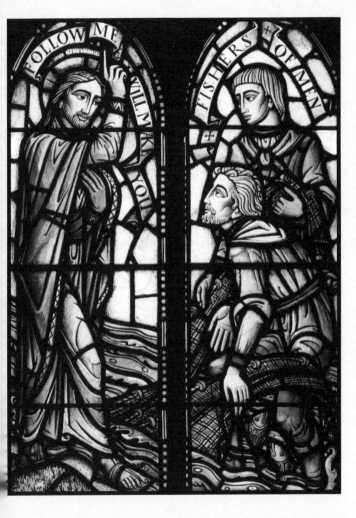

Jesus calls Peter

This extraordinary story shows that the mercy of God can be found in the ordinary events of our daily lives. Jesus meets these fishermen when he is preaching around the Sea of Galilee. They had just finished their night's work, and caught nothing. The story of the great catch of fish is quite inexplicable. How was it that they had had no success all night, but suddenly there was an enormous catch of fish?

The real miracle, the really extraordinary event, is in the life of Simon Peter. His life is suddenly transformed and he becomes the first disciple called by Jesus.

Peter is aware of his sins and mistakes. 'I am a sinful man,' he says. Nevertheless, Jesus has chosen him for a special task. This gospel of mercy suggests that we are all called, and that the unworthiness we feel does not stop God from loving us, calling us, and keeping faith with us. Peter was so struck by this that, through thick and thin, he stayed with Jesus, even in really tough times.

Not only Peter, but James and John also, are called by Jesus. Something about the actions and words of Jesus led them to leave everything and follow him. In the everyday events of life God can suddenly call us to change, and give us the strength we need to take an entirely new path.

• Have there been moments in your life when a new way was suddenly opened, and how did you react?

• Has awareness of sins and failings ever stopped you from moving on? It did not stop Simon Peter.

3

The Challenge of Mercy

LUKE 6:27-30, 36-37

Jesus said: 'I say this to you who are listening: Love your enemies, do good to those who hate you, bless those who curse you, pray for those who treat you badly. To the man who takes your cloak from you, do not refuse your tunic. Give to everyone who asks you, and do not ask for your property back from the man who robs you. Be compassionate as your Father is compassionate. Do not judge, and you will not be judged yourselves; do not condemn, and you will not be condemned yourselves; grant pardon and you will be pardoned.'

The Challenge of Mercy

Mercy is a major theme in the Gospel of Luke. It is shown in the outreach of Jesus to those who fail, to the poor and the sick. But it is also seen in his teaching, and, through this teaching, the challenge to be merciful comes to us. The words here are directed to the disciples of Jesus, not just those who were his contemporaries, like Peter, James and John, but also to us, who hear his teaching today. The challenge of mercy is directed to us.

This passage is very similar to the teaching in the Sermon on the Mount, which is found in the Gospel of Matthew. Here in Luke the location is less clear: crowds have gathered to hear Jesus on what is described as 'a piece of level ground'.

'I say this to you,' begins Jesus. His teaching is different, different in content and different in tone. While earlier teachers had said 'love your neighbour, and hate your enemy', Jesus invites love of enemies. Here we see how the Christian gospel challenges our human inclinations and our behaviour. And yet, with these words we discover what it is to be truly human: to love God with all our heart, and all people as brothers and sisters.

There are a series of reversals of what we might be inclined to do: do good to those who hate you, bless those who curse you, pray for those who abuse you.

The words of Jesus reach a climax when he says: 'Be compassionate as your Father is compassionate.' Astounding as it may seem, we are invited to be like God, and to be like God in what is God's most tender and loving characteristic, mercy.

There is a widespread misunderstanding that the God of Jews and Christians is more than anything a god of condemnation and punishment. And yet throughout the Bible, in both Old and New Testaments, God emerges as a loving god, who forgives, and whose mercy endures for ever. This is confirmed by Jesus, both by his teaching and by his actions.

- Is it really possible to love your enemies? Recall the times that you did so, and resolve to do so again.

- Be compassionate and merciful, as God is! Reflect on this extraordinary challenge, and just do it, with the grace of God!

4

Forgiveness and Love

LUKE 7:36-37, 44-48, 50

One of the Pharisees invited Jesus to a meal. When he arrived and took his place at table, a woman came in, who was a sinner in the town. She had heard he was dining with the Pharisee and had brought with her an alabaster jar of ointment. She waited behind him at his feet, weeping, and her tears fell on his feet, and she wiped them away with her hair; then she covered his feet with kisses and anointed them with the ointment.

Then he turned to the woman and said to the Pharisee, 'Simon, you see this woman? I came into your house, and you poured no water over my feet, but she has poured out her tears over my feet and wiped them away with her hair. You gave me no kiss, but she has been covering my feet with kisses ever since I came in. You did not anoint my head with oil, but she has anointed my feet with ointment. For this reason I tell you that her sins, her many sins, must have been forgiven her, or she would not have shown such great love. It is the man who is forgiven little who shows little love.' Then he said to her, 'Your sins are forgiven. Your faith has saved you; go in peace.'

Forgiveness and Love

In this gospel passage, we see once again the power of mercy to change lives. The woman had a reputation, and she knew it. Peter had described himself as 'a sinner' when Jesus called him. This woman is known as 'a sinner' in the town. We know no more of her past. What we see is someone who seizes the opportunity for change, and expresses in the most tender way her gratitude for the new start she has been offered.

Jesus draws a comparison between the woman, and her extravagant demonstration of love for him, and the Pharisee named Simon, who is courteous and proper in his behaviour, but shows no such depth of love in welcoming Jesus.

How was it that the woman had the energy to change? This was to be no passing fad, but a wholesale and profound new direction in her life. What was it that brought her to Simon's house to gate-crash the party he was throwing for Jesus? Surely she must have heard what Jesus had been preaching, and that he offered forgiveness to all, especially to those who were despised and rejected in the society of his day.

The forgiveness she has already embraced is confirmed for her by Jesus. Her sins are truly forgiven. This new chance is real. Her faith has saved her. She leaves the party in peace.

• How can the offer of new life through Jesus bring forgiveness to your heart?

• What does this woman say to you? Can you too grab God's offer of forgiveness and follow Jesus in a life of loving service?

5

The Good Samaritan

LUKE 10:29-37

A lawyer said to Jesus, 'Who is my neighbour?' Jesus replied, 'A man was once on his way down from Jerusalem to Jericho and fell into the hands of brigands; they took all he had, beat him and then made off, leaving him half dead. Now a priest happened to be travelling down the same road, but when he saw the man, he passed by on the other side. In the same way a Levite who came to the place saw him, and passed by on the other side. But a Samaritan traveller who came upon him was moved with compassion when he saw him. He went up and bandaged his wounds, pouring oil and wine on them. He then lifted him on to his own mount, carried him to the inn and looked after him. Next day, he took out two denarii and handed them to the innkeeper. 'Look after him,' he said, 'and on my way back I will make good any extra expense you have.' Which of these three, do you think, proved himself a neighbour to the man who fell into the brigands' hands?' 'The one who took pity on him,' replied the lawyer. Jesus said to him, 'Go, and do the same yourself.'

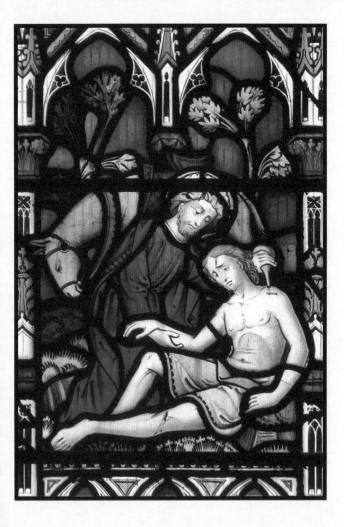

The Good Samaritan

As the gospel of Luke progresses Jesus begins his journey to Jerusalem, a journey to the place where he will be put to death. During this journey Luke records some of the finest teaching of Jesus, and some parables, stories illustrating his teaching, which are only found in this gospel and have been treasured through the centuries by people of all faiths and none.

The parable of the Good Samaritan is one such. This is mercy in action. Mercy is often practised by those from whom you least expect it. The religious individuals, the priest, and the Levite, an employee of the temple busy with his religious duties, both fail to show mercy. It is the Samaritan, a member of a community who lived apart from the regular Jewish believers, who is truly compassionate.

He was moved with compassion when he saw him. His reaction is immediate, bandaging wounds, pouring oil and wine, seating him on his donkey, taking him to a place of shelter, and even providing for his future care and recovery.

Go and do the same yourself, says Jesus. Be a neighbour to those in need. Show compassion in the simplest of ways. For Jesus all people are neighbours, and all can show mercy.

• Thank God for all the opportunities you have to be a good Samaritan to those in need.

• What is there to stop you from being compassionate as God is compassionate?

6

The Barren Fig Tree

LUKE 13:6-9

Jesus told this parable: 'A man had a fig tree planted in his vineyard, and he came looking for fruit on it but found none. He said to the man who looked after the vineyard, 'Look here, for three years now I have been coming to look for fruit on this fig tree and finding none. Cut it down: why should it be taking up the ground?' 'Sir,' the man replied, 'leave it one more year and give me time to dig round it and manure it: it may bear fruit next year; if not, then you can cut it down.'"

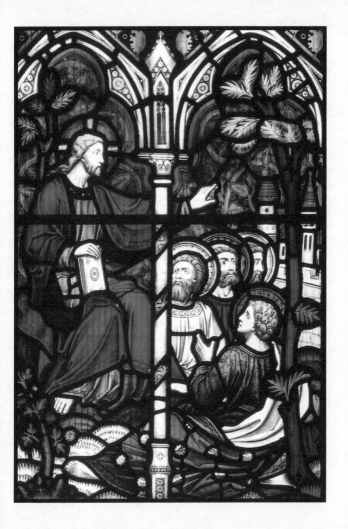

The Barren Fig Tree

This parable is not so well known, but it has a powerful message. This is indeed a parable of mercy. The fruitless fig tree is a symbol. The Bible often speaks of people not bearing fruit, not fulfilling their potential.

While the owner of the garden is inclined to take drastic action, the gardener has compassion. The story has often been understood as pointing to the patient mercy of Christ.

How often in our lives do we need time to learn and time to change! Jesus understands this. His teaching recalls what the prophets and the psalms of the Old Testament repeatedly teach. God is merciful. God waits for people to come to their senses and respond. God is described as 'slow to anger, and rich in mercy'.

The parable ends rather abruptly. This story does not tell us the reaction of the man who owned the vineyard. Did he agree to the gardener's request, or did he tell him to cut the tree down immediately?

It is important to understand this rather puzzling element in the story. God is merciful indeed, but human beings living in time have a short time on earth to recognise the goodness of God, and to change. The distressing situation of people who might have developed their potential for good, and did nothing, is perhaps what lies at the heart of this parable.

God is patient. God waits. Human beings are free, but we have limited time. There is an urgent need to hear the good news and respond to it.

• Are you the kind of person who puts off really important decisions? What is stopping you from responding to the good news of God's mercy?

• Do you give others time to change?

7

The Prodigal Son

LUKE 15:17-24

Jesus said: 'The younger son came to his senses and said, 'How many of my father's paid servants have more food than they want, and here am I dying of hunger! I will leave this place and go to my father and say: Father, I have sinned against heaven and against you; I no longer deserve to be called your son; treat me as one of your paid servants.' So he left the place and went back to his father.

'While he was still a long way off, his father saw him and was moved with pity. He ran to the boy, clasped him in his arms and kissed him tenderly. Then his son said, 'Father, I have sinned against heaven and against you. I no longer deserve to be called your son.' But the father said to his servants, 'Quick! Bring out the best robe and put it on him; put a ring on his finger and sandals on his feet. Bring the calf we have been fattening and kill it; we are going to have a feast, a celebration, because this son of mine was dead and has come back to life; he was lost and is found.''

The Prodigal Son

This is a section of a very famous parable, known generally as 'The Prodigal Son'. A man has two sons. The younger decides to leave home and wastes his inheritance in a life of pleasure. Our passage begins when he comes to his senses. He trusts his father enough to return, and his trust is rewarded.

The father is the embodiment of mercy. As soon as his son comes to his senses, and decides to try to put things right, there is no hesitation from his father. The warm embrace and determination to celebrate say it all.

But there is another person in the story. The elder son is out in the fields, working as usual. When he finds out what has happened, he is angry with his father. 'All these years I have slaved for you and never disobeyed you,' he says. His father speaks tenderly to him: 'My son, you are with me always, and all I have is yours.' As the story ends we do not know whether the elder son has the heart to welcome back his brother, and imitate the father's love.

This parable features three individuals, each with a powerful message. The prodigal son tells us about the possibility of a new start. The father teaches us about readiness to forgive. The elder son warns us about stubbornness of heart when we see others forgiven.

• Do you resent mercy being shown to others, while welcoming it for yourself?

• To whom might you too show mercy? Has it been a long time coming? Might now be the time?

8

The Pharisee and
the Tax Collector

LUKE 18:9-14

Jesus spoke the following parable to some people who prided themselves on being virtuous and despised everyone else. 'Two men went up to the Temple to pray, one a Pharisee, the other a tax collector. The Pharisee stood there and said this prayer to himself, 'I thank you, God, that I am not grasping, unjust, adulterous like the rest of mankind, and particularly that I am not like this tax collector here. I fast twice a week; I pay tithes on all I get.' The tax collector stood some distance away, not daring even to raise his eyes to heaven; but he beat his breast and said, 'God, be merciful to me, a sinner.' This man, I tell you, went home again at rights with God; the other did not. For everyone who exalts himself will be humbled, but the man who humbles himself will be exalted.'

The Pharisee and
the Tax Collector

This story may well raise a smile. Does anyone really pray like this Pharisee is supposed to have prayed? Jesus' description of the Pharisee, who belonged to a religious group who were known for their dedication to God and to the needs of the common people, is a bit of a caricature. The point of the parable is the contrast between the Pharisee's pride, which discounts any failings and sins, and the tax collector's sense of his unworthiness, which makes him forget any good he might have done.

The one places himself in full view of everyone in order to vaunt himself. The other keeps his distance and lowers his gaze.

God delights in showing mercy, but our human hearts must be open to receive that mercy. Like Simon Peter, like the woman who was a sinner, like the prodigal son, we need to recognise our need of that mercy.

Jesus says that one went home justified, while the other did not. The tax collector had opened his heart to the mercy of God, while the Pharisee did not recognise his need for it.

The prophets of Israel, called to preach the truth to the people of God in the centuries before Christ, would frequently challenge those who practised religious observance of all kinds, and yet neglected to practise justice, kindness and compassion for the poor. Jesus joins this long line of prophets who preached the truth. They were unafraid to challenge people, particularly the religious people who considered themselves better than others. It was the religious leaders who would plot the downfall of Jesus.

• Would you consider yourself to be like the Pharisee or like the tax collector? What stops you from being honest with yourself?

• Which of the two prayers the two men say in the parable sits more comfortably with you? Which one is more open to the gift of God's mercy?

9

Zacchaeus Meets Jesus

LUKE 19:1-10

Jesus entered Jericho and was going through the town when a man whose name was Zacchaeus made his appearance; he was one of the senior tax collectors and a wealthy man. He was anxious to see what kind of man Jesus was, but he was too short and could not see him for the crowd; so he ran ahead and climbed a sycamore tree to catch a glimpse of Jesus who was to pass that way. When Jesus reached the spot he looked up and spoke to him: 'Zacchaeus, come down. Hurry, because I must stay at your house today.' And he hurried down and welcomed him joyfully. They all complained when they saw what was happening. 'He has gone to stay at a sinner's house,' they said. But Zacchaeus stood his ground and said to the Lord, 'Look, sir, I am going to give half my property to the poor, and if I have cheated anybody I will pay him back four times the amount.' And Jesus said to him, 'Today salvation has come to this house, because this man too is a son of Abraham; for the Son of Man has come to seek out and save what was lost.'

Zaccheus Meets Jesus

Just as the woman who was a sinner was determined to reach Jesus, so Zaccheus overcomes all the obstacles to present himself before the Lord. Both have heard the good news and act on it. Zaccheus was a tax collector, and an important one. Tax collectors often abused their power to line their own pockets. But Zaccheus senses the chance of a new start, and is willing to climb a tree to embrace it. The friendly words of Jesus, which speak of God's mercy, are sufficient to change his heart, and he commits himself to making amends and to repaying what he has stolen with interest.

But there are those who complain. That Jesus shares the hospitality of sinners is a cause of annoyance to the virtuous. They cannot approve of the new start offered to Zaccheus. They are scandalised that Jesus invites himself into the sinner's house.

This passage ends with a solemn declaration by Jesus: today salvation has come to the house of Zaccheus. Jesus, who brings good news to the poor, has come 'to seek out and save what was lost'. Like the prodigal son, Zaccheus was dead and has come back to life. He was lost and is found.

• What do you think made Zacchaeus so determined to meet Jesus? Could you share his enthusiasm?

• Zacchaeus shows it is possible to wipe the slate clean and to begin again. Are there any parts of your life which need such attention?

10

Peter's Denials and Reconciliation

LUKE 22:54-62

They seized Jesus and led him away, and they took him to the high priest's house. Peter followed at a distance. They had lit a fire in the middle of the courtyard and Peter sat down among them, and as he was sitting there by the blaze a servant-girl saw him, peered at him and said, 'This person was with him too.' But he denied it. 'Woman,' he said, 'I do not know him.' Shortly afterwards someone else saw him and said, 'You are another of them.' But Peter replied, 'I am not, my friend.' About an hour later another man insisted, saying, 'This fellow was certainly with him. Why, he is a Galilean.' 'My friend,' said Peter, 'I do not know what you are talking about.' At that instant, while he was still speaking, the cock crew, and the Lord turned and looked straight at Peter, and Peter remembered what the Lord had said to him, 'Before the cock crows today, you will have disowned me three times.' And he went outside and wept bitterly.

Peter's Denials and Reconciliation

At the last supper the disciples had shared with Jesus earlier in the evening Jesus had spoken of the difficulty Peter would later face. Amid all Peter's protestations of loyalty, Jesus announced Peter's coming denials, which would happen 'before the cock crows' to herald the approach of dawn. But Jesus also foresaw that Peter would recover and then be able to 'strengthen his brothers'.

Our gospel passage reports how Peter did indeed, later that night, once Jesus had been arrested, deny his friendship with Jesus, out of understandable fear and terror at the prospect of being arrested just like Jesus. The account of Peter's denials grows in intensity as the servant girl, another person, and a third challenge him. But the tension is suddenly broken.

Even while he is still denying his knowledge of Jesus, the cock crows. It is then that 'the Lord turned and looked straight at Peter'. What was happening to Jesus must have been visible from the courtyard. Peter could see Jesus, and this is what saves Peter and brings him to his senses. Jesus' gaze is surely not one of reproach, but one of compassion and understanding. What Peter did was spontaneous and natural, though lacking courage. This event will change Peter, and his own sense of failure and subsequent reconciliation will give him strength and the stature to strengthen others, just as Jesus had said.

• Have you ever been gripped by such fear that you denied what was true?

• How have experiences of weakness ultimately helped you to know yourself, to know God's mercy, and to show mercy to others?

11

Jesus Speaks from the Cross

LUKE 23:33-43

When they reached the place called The Skull, they crucified Jesus there and the two criminals also, one on the right, the other on the left. Jesus said, 'Father, forgive them; they do not know what they are doing.' Then they cast lots to share out his clothing. The people stayed there watching him. As for the leaders, they jeered at him. 'He saved others,' they said, 'let him save himself if he is the Christ of God, the Chosen One.' The soldiers mocked him too, and when they approached to offer him vinegar they said, 'If you are the king of the Jews save yourself.' Above him there was an inscription: 'This is the King of the Jews.'

One of the criminals hanging there abused him. 'Are you not the Christ?' he said. 'Save yourself and us as well.' But the other spoke up and rebuked him, 'Have you no fear of God at all?' he said. 'You got the same sentence as he did, but in our case we deserved it: we are paying for what we did. But this man has done nothing wrong. Jesus,' he said, 'remember me when you come into your kingdom.' 'Indeed, I promise you,' Jesus replied, 'today you will be with me in paradise.'

Jesus Speaks from the Cross

Jesus has made his way painfully after torture to the place of execution. His first words from the cross are nevertheless words of peace and of God's mercy. He asks forgiveness for those who are doing such injustice. The soldiers are intent on getting what they can for themselves and cast lots on his clothing.

There is a fevered condemnation of Jesus from those who witness his crucifixion. People taunt him, turning his preaching of love, and his saving healings into insults and derision: 'he saved others, let him save himself.'

One of the two criminals crucified with him follows the crowd. He too derides the claims made for Jesus that he is God's anointed. How could God's anointed come to this? And yet, this is the heart of the gospel message, that the one sent by God would be a victim of cruelty and injustice, and yet be raised and vindicated by God.

There is one voice of truth amid all the mayhem. Once again it comes from an unexpected source. Just as the good Samaritan showed mercy and kindness, just as the woman who was a sinner had the greatest insight into mercy and love, just as Zacchaeus was more enthusiastic than all his fellows to hear the words of Jesus, so here it is the 'good thief' who trusts in the possibility of being saved despite his criminal past. His words, 'Jesus, remember me, when you come into your kingdom,' are a source of comfort. Jesus' words of reply offer hope and reassurance, 'Today you will be with me in paradise.'

• Do you go with the crowd in unthinking judgement and condemnation?

• Do you speak up for the truth, for goodness, mercy and a new start?

12

Jesus Risen from the Dead
Speaks to the Disciples

LUKE 24:44-49

Jesus told them, 'This is what I meant when I said, while I was still with you, that everything written about me in the Law of Moses, in the Prophets and in the Psalms, has to be fulfilled.' He then opened their minds to understand the Scriptures, and he said to them, 'So you see how it is written that the Christ would suffer and on the third day rise from the dead, and that, in his name, repentance for the forgiveness of sins would be preached to all the nations, beginning from Jerusalem. You are witnesses to this. And now I am sending down to you what the Father has promised. Stay in the city then, until you are clothed with the power from on high.'

Jesus Risen from the Dead
Speaks to the Disciples

Before the gospel ends, the risen Jesus helps the disciples to understand the extraordinary events which they have witnessed, and sends them out to preach to the ends of the earth. It is the conviction of Christians that the Scriptures prepare for the coming of Jesus Christ, as well as for his death and resurrection. This is why Christians cherish the Bible, including as it does the books of the Jewish faith to which Jesus refers here.

Fulfilment means that the hopes expressed in the earlier Scriptures have been realised, and in a way which far surpasses expectations. Jesus opens the minds of the disciples so that they can explain to others the meaning of the events they have lived through.

The message they will preach involves change, and it involves the mercy of God. The new start which we have seen experienced by so many individuals in the Gospel of Luke is available to all. Sinfulness is no barrier, for a new start can be made with the mercy of God. This message is to be preached 'to all nations, beginning from Jerusalem'. The gospel message will go beyond the land of Jesus and reach the ends of the earth.

The essential gospel message is that God is the God of all, who cares deeply for creation, and who allows a new start. Reading these gospels of mercy may well have suggested to you ways of beginning again, or of making changes in your life. The gospel is not called 'good news' for nothing. It really is a message of God's love for all, which makes extraordinary things possible.

• How have you reacted to the gospel passages which announce in their various ways the mercy of God?

• How can Jesus bring new wisdom, new confidence and new vigour to your life?

Picture credits

Courtesy of © Fr Lawrence Lew, OP

Page 5: Bath Abbey

Page 9: All Saints' church in St Andrews

Page 13: Church of SS Gervais & Protais in Paris.

Page 21: Buckland parish church

Page 25: Ely Cathedral

Page 29: St Mary Abbott, in Kensington, London

Page 33: St Gregory's parish church, Tredington

Page 41: Witney parish church

Page 37: Saint-Pierre in Neuilly-sur-Seine

Page 17: BasPhoto / Shutterstock.com

Page 45: Cathedral of Bayeux, Normandy, France.
© Jorisvo / Shutterstock.com

Page 49: Roger de Montfort / Shutterstock.com

Mercy: The Greatest Gift

Meeting the Love of Christ

Barbara Reed Mason

Pope Francis's call for a Holy Year of Mercy begins with a call to spiritual conversion in each of us. What are the spiritual and tangible aspects of mercy? Many Christians today can be unaware that we can keep the supernatural life within us vigorous by engaging with the spiritual works of mercy. This is not a matter of just being good to others only, but of our own salvation. Saint John Paul II said that the greatest gift of mercy is bringing people to savour Christ's love.

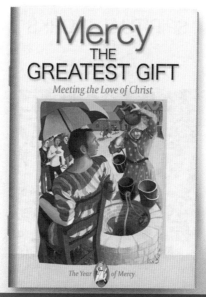

SP47   ISBN 978 1 78469 093 9

Spiritual Works of Mercy

Mgr Paul Grogan

Most Christians want to live an active faith yet feel perplexed about how to do so. The seven interconnected 'spiritual works of mercy' come to our aid: counselling the doubtful; instructing the ignorant; admonishing sinners; comforting the afflicted; forgiving offences; bearing wrongs patiently; and praying for the living and the dead. Through such acts of mercy we can respond fully to God's goodness towards us, involving conversion of our interior life: such acts are truly God's acts of mercy; we, mere human agents for God to alleviate people's unhappiness.

SP46   ISBN 978 1 78469 087 8

Corporal Works of Mercy
Mercy in Action
Mgr Richard Atherton

Feeding the hungry and thirsty, clothing the naked, housing the homeless, visiting the imprisoned, visiting the sick, and burying the dead - Pope Francis wants us to stop and think again, especially during the Year of Mercy. Are these things I can do, or are they for others to get on with? What good do they do? Actions of mercy are often terribly ordinary and doable. Mgr Atherton guides us through the spiritual and practical matters that Love asks of all Christians.

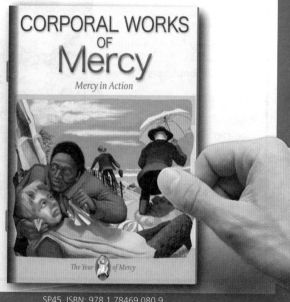

SP45 ISBN: 978 1 78469 080 9

A world of Catholic reading at your fingertips...

Catholic Faith, Life & Truth for all

CTS
www.CTSbooks.org

twitter: @CTSpublishers

facebook.com/CTSpublishers

Catholic Truth Society, Publishers to the Holy See.